IT'S TIME TO EAT RAMBUTANS

It's Time to Eat RAMBUTANS

Walter the Educator

Silent King Books
A WhichHead Entertainment Imprint

Copyright © 2025 by Walter the Educator

All rights reserved. No part of this book may be reproduced in any manner whatsoever without written per- mission except in the case of brief quotations embodied in critical articles and reviews.

First Printing, 2024

Disclaimer

This book is a literary work; the story is not about specific persons, locations, situations, and/or circumstances unless mentioned in a historical context. Any resemblance to real persons, locations, situations, and/or circumstances is coincidental. This book is for entertainment and informational purposes only. The author and publisher offer this information without warranties expressed or implied. No matter the grounds, neither the author nor the publisher will be accountable for any losses, injuries, or other damages caused by the reader's use of this book. The use of this book acknowledges an understanding and acceptance of this disclaimer.

It's Time to Eat RAMBUTANS is a collectible early learning book by Walter the Educator suitable for all ages belonging to Walter the Educator's Time to Eat Book Series. Collect more books at WaltertheEducator.com

USE THE EXTRA SPACE TO TAKE NOTES AND DOCUMENT YOUR MEMORIES

RAMBUTANS

Rambutan time is here, hooray!

It's Time to Eat
Rambutans

The spiky fruit is on display.

Its skin is red, with hairs so fine,

A jungle treat that's just divine!

We pluck them ripe, right from the tree,

A fuzzy fruit for you and me.

The spikes are soft, so have no fear,

Rambutan season brings us cheer.

We give it a twist, the shell pops wide,

And there's the treasure tucked inside.

Its flesh is white, so smooth and sweet,

A juicy, tasty fruit to eat.

It smells so fresh, a gentle breeze,

It's like a hug from tropical trees.

With every bite, the flavor flows,

The joy of rambutans surely shows.

It's Time to Eat
Rambutans

The seed inside is shiny brown,

We spit it out, it tumbles down.

The fruit's the part we love to chew,

So sweet and soft, like morning dew.

We share it round with friends so dear,

A spiky treat to bring good cheer.

The rambutan, a funny sight,

Brings smiles to faces, pure delight!

You'll love it fresh, or in a dish,

Rambutans grant your fruity wish.

In smoothies too, they're just so sweet,

A snack that simply can't be beat.

The tree that grows them stands so tall,

Its branches hold the prize for all.

Let's thank the sun, the rain, the air,

It's Time to Eat
Rambutans

For rambutans, beyond compare.

We giggle as we munch away,

This fruity treat has made our day.

With sticky hands and happy cheer,

We'll eat them up, then wait next year.

So when you see the spiky red,

Remember all the fun you've had.

It's rambutan time, shout hooray,

It's Time to Eat
Rambutans

The yummiest fruit in every way!

ABOUT THE CREATOR

Walter the Educator is one of the pseudonyms for Walter Anderson. Formally educated in Chemistry, Business, and Education, he is an educator, an author, a diverse entrepreneur, and he is the son of a disabled war veteran. "Walter the Educator" shares his time between educating and creating. He holds interests and owns several creative projects that entertain, enlighten, enhance, and educate, hoping to inspire and motivate you. Follow, find new works, and stay up to date with Walter the Educator™

at WaltertheEducator.com

www.ingramcontent.com/pod-product-compliance
Lightning Source LLC
LaVergne TN
LVHW052014060526
838201LV00059B/4030